A LAYMAN'S THOUGHTS

On The Gospel of John

DAVID M. EAKIN

LifeRich Publishing is a registered trademark of The Reader's Digest Association, Inc.

LifeRich Publishing books may be ordered through booksellers or by contacting:

LifeRich Publishing
1663 Liberty Drive
Bloomington, IN 47403
www.liferichpublishing.com
1 (888) 238-8637

Because of the dynamic nature of the Internet, any web addresses or links contained in this book may have changed since publication and may no longer be valid. The views expressed in this work are solely those of the author and do not necessarily reflect the views of the publisher, and the publisher hereby disclaims any responsibility for them.

Any people depicted in stock imagery provided by Getty Images are models, and such images are being used for illustrative purposes only.
Certain stock imagery © Getty Images.

Scripture quotations are from the New Revised Standard Version Bible, copyright © 1989 the Division of Christian Education of the National Council of the Churches of Christ in the United States of America. Used by permission. All rights reserved.

ISBN: 978-1-4897-2944-6 (sc)
ISBN: 978-1-4897-2943-9 (hc)
ISBN: 978-1-4897-2987-3 (e)

Library of Congress Control Number: 2020913384

Print information available on the last page.

LifeRich Publishing rev. date: 07/29/2020

A LAYMAN'S THOUGHTS

On The Gospel of John

John 1 is such a miraculous chapter to stop and dwell on for a few minutes. "In the beginning". As we start the first chapter of John we can think of Genesis 1 as we discover the creation of all that exists. Here in John 1 we see creation as well as an implication of the trinity just as we see in Genesis 1.

Let us consider Genesis 1 discussing the creation, the 1st chapter of Matthew discussing the human birth of our Savior, the 1st Chapter of John showing the divinity of and the 1st chapter of Revelation describing the majesty and glory of the risen, resurrected and ascended Anointed One.

John 1 reveals Christ as the Word, the expression of God, the love of God for His people and the glory of Christ now and forever. How can we read this chapter and not be awed by the power, love and majesty of the One who came to save us and to make us children of God? In doing so He not only saves us but resides in our hearts through the Holy Spirit.

It goes on to say that Christ came unto His own and His own did not receive Him. The Creator came to those He created, and the Author of Life was rejected by those He created. Their eyes were shut and their hearts were closed. How could this be? How could they, how could we, not see Him for who He is?

Then this chapter goes on in verse 12 to say that He gawwve to those who received Him the right to become children of God.

When Philip told Nathanael about Jesus and Nathanael doubted, Philip said "come and see".

I say now, come and see. Are we in danger at times of shutting Him out today? Do we ignore the Author of Life? Do we forget to spend time with the One who created us, redeemed us, and sustains us? Do we forget to thank Him for our salvation and His spirit within us? Do we forget to spend time with our closest Friend whose presence is with us?

I say again, Come and See.

Prayer: Savior, thank You for coming to those you made, even to be rejected, so that by Your death and resurrection, you could restore us as Your friend. You have given us your Spirit. May we always take time to realize who You are and what You have done for us.

Help us to "come and see" and to invite others to see you as well. Amen.

It is interesting that John records the first sign or miracle performed by Jesus as the time He changed water into wine at the wedding. We may ask why this is important. What significance is this? It's just a wedding after all.

John uses the word "sign" for a reason. This miracle was a sign. A sign of what? A sign of His divinity, His creative power, His control over creation. Let us remember what John said in the first chapter. Jesus was the Word and "the Word was with God and the Word was God". He created everything. This sign points to Christ as the Word, as God. Jesus came to earth, to His creation and to His people. The Creator came to us. As God, He has control over all that was created.

This also shows that God does indeed work in the lives of His people for His purposes. In this case the miracle was a sign of Christ's divinity and His power over His creation.

Prayer: Jesus, sometimes in our own lives we picture You as merely human or at sometimes tend to think of You in merely human terms. But You are God and through you all was created. And yet you came to save us. To die for us. To raise us up with you from death. You love us and care about us and our lives here on earth.

Lord, help us always to see Your love for us in our lives on earth and forevermore. Amen.

Jesus, comparatively uneducated in human terms, speaks to a Jewish religious leader. A learned man. A leader who knew the Old Testament, including the prophesies. Yet this leader was in a sense blind and Jesus had to explain the truth to Nicodemus, who came to him at night and in secret. Jesus talks with him about newness of life. He talks of a new birth.

Jesus has burst into human history for a reason.

This may seem odd but perhaps we should think of Christmas. Why? Because Jesus came to die for us, be resurrected and ascended so we can live with Him now and forever. This truth has burst into the world and it is real. Christ gave Himself so, as it says in verse 15, "that whoever believes may in Him have eternal life" (NASB)

John 3:16 is called the Gospel in a nutshell. "For God so loved the world that He gave His only begotten Son that whosoever believes in Him should not perish, but have eternal life" (NASB).

Why so often do we go about our busy lives without acknowledging Him? We often let life stream by, getting caught up in so many things without even a thought of our Savior who created us to live with Him.

Prayer: Lord Jesus, burst upon us in the realization of the magnitude of Your love for us. Help us not take the gospel for granted because it reveals your love for us yesterday, today and tomorrow. You are the center of all human history.

Come Lord Jesus. Amen.

In this chapter, we again see Jesus bursting in the world He created. We see him with the woman at the well. While the Jews generally despised the Samaritans, he spoke with the Samaritan woman and revealed Himself as the Messiah.

Jesus stays with the Samaritans for 2 days longer and many believed in Him. At first, they came to see Jesus because of the woman's testimony but they came to believe "because of His word" (NASB). He came to them, He revealed Himself to them and stayed among them.

Jesus heals the royal official's son. The official believed Jesus when He told him to go home because his son was alive and would live. He burst into the life of the royal official. He again shows His power over creation and even death itself.

Let Him burst into our lives and change us forever.

Prayer: Jesus, burst into our life today. Reveal Yourself to us anew and help us to realize the Your personal presence in our daily life.

Lord, help us to understand the breadth and depth of Your love for us and that You are with us no matter what is going on around us. Amen.

Chapter 5 begins with another sign or miracle. Again, we see Jesus personally changing the life of someone who did not know Him. We do not know what the "sickness" (NASB) was but we know the individual could not walk because he told Jesus he had no one to help put him in the healing waters. Jesus did not have to help the man into the water. He simply told him to rise and take up his pallet, which was a bed for the poor.

First, we see that Jesus healed the man. He has the power over creation, life and death.

Secondly, we see the man did not argue with Jesus but obeyed. Sometimes, we pray and we argue with Jesus about the healing He wants to bring to us. Whether it is in terms of health, emotions, relationships, He provides restoration with and through Him. However often we are afraid, we are scared, we are used to our condition. Sometimes we want to stay in our condition because we have begun to be comfortable with the condition. Perhaps we fear change, even if it means healing. Let us "arise" and "walk". Let us allow Jesus to change our lives.

Next, we see the religious rulers wanted to kill Jesus, which is against the 10 commandments, because He healed on the Sabbath and called God His Father. How hardened their hearts must have been. May it never be so for us.

Finally, let us note that Jesus even says that he did "nothing of Himself" but only what the Father does. He was in such unity with the Father. Let us remember He died for us so we can also have unity with Him and the Father. May we do nothing on our own accord but that which we do out of our unity with Him, at His direction, on His path.

Prayer: Jesus, we need Your healing. We are broken. Provide for healing and help us to rise and walk with You from this day forward. May your healing change our lives forever and may we obey your command to rise and live in your healing. Bring us ever closer to You each day. You desire our companionship. You died for our salvation.

Live in our hearts so we may live in unity with You now and forevermore. Amen.

Most people read John 6 and talk about Jesus feeding the 5 thousand with 2 fish and 5 loaves or Jesus walking on the water.

Remember, His "signs" are a springboard to greater truths.

In further teaching, Jesus knows the needs of the heart and soul of men and women and tells us in verse 27 not to work for food that perishes but "for the food which endures to eternal life which the Son of Man shall give you…." (NASB).

This reminds me of Matthew 6:33: "But seek first His kingdom and His righteousness; and all these things will be added to you." (NASB)

Let us remember that the God fed the Israelites, His chosen people, in the wilderness after He delivered them from Egypt.

Remember, the apostle Paul said he had learned to be content whether he had plenty or was in need. Why could he say that? How could he say that?

If we are His children, will He not provide for us?

We get so busy with life, work, kids, church, activities, we begin to run on automatic. We just go through life, perhaps we simply get through the day.

We sometimes forget to take a deep breath and remember the most important, basic part of life. Christ loved us so much that he came to earth and died for our sins. Yes, He loves us and died for us so we could live with Him today and forever. He wants us to live that life with Him beginning now. He wants a continued, daily relationship with us. He wants our love, affection and friendship. Yes, the eternal God wants our companionship.

Prayer: *Lord, we thank you for your companionship. Help us to give ourselves afresh to You today. In this busy life, help us to remember our greatest love is for the One who loved us first. Thank you for your companionship.*

May we love You and serve You today. Amen.

It always strikes me that the leaders of God's chosen people sought to silence and even kill the one Son of God, through whom all that exists was created. God sent His Son to His people and the leaders of His own people rejected Him.

I sometimes ask myself who I would have followed had I lived at that time in history. I would like to think I would have been a close follower of Jesus and wish I could see Him face to face. How it would be wonderful to sit down at the kitchen table in person and have a personal conversation, to say "I love You in person.

Then I remember how flawed I am and that I tend to be a rather conventional personality. Would I have been one of tradition and followed the Jewish leaders at the time or gone with who appeared at the time to be a radical, this Jesus who did signs and wonders even though the conventional religious leaders did not recognize him?

In verse 12 we see that there were those speaking in the crowd that Jesus was a good man and others were saying He was leading them astray. Verse 31 said many believed He was the Christ. Verse 40 shows some referred to Him as the Prophet. The religious leaders mocked those that followed Him. Who would I have followed? If I had lived at that time, what would I have said of Jesus?

We come to the question: Who do you and I say Jesus is? Is He simply a good man or someone leading people astray from the conventional, religious or worldly "wise" views of today? Or, is He the very Son of God worthy of our hearts, minds and souls? Is He one who is worthy of not only our worship but of giving our very selves?

If we accept Him in our hearts as the Son of God and the center of our lives, how do we live? Are we sharing His love with those around us? Do we care for those hurting, who are hungry, who need a word of encouragement, who need our love day in and day out, even when we sometimes think we can give no more? Perhaps we feel we can't give any more but Christ in us has unlimited love and unlimited strength that He wants to share through us.

Prayer: *Lord, help me to examine my heart today and humbly ask You to reveal not only my own lack of ability to believe on my own accord but the unlimited power to believe and act that You give. After all, You love us so much that You died for us. May I love you more today and make You the center of my life. Help me to realize more tangibly that You saved me and You want to reside with me fully.*

Help me to share your gospel, the "Good News", with the world in word and deed. Amen.

Jesus said, "If you are Abraham's children, do the deeds of Abraham". Yet these same "spiritual" leaders where actually seeking an opportunity to kill Him.

Abraham was a person of faith who we should all admire and try to imitate. He believed God. He followed God's path and His instructions without hesitation. The history of Abraham is one we should all keep in mind and study more. We should strive to follow His example.

However, the Jewish leaders, who knew the prophecies and were looking for the Savior, did not believe. Rather, they disobeyed their own commandments by seeking kill Him, who was in fact their own Savior. They did not understand their own prophecies. Perhaps they feared losing their own power and station as privileged ones. Perhaps their own zeal for conventionality caused their own blindness to see the truth.

The Jewish leaders stated that they were free but they were blind. They were Abraham's children physically but were not Abraham's children spiritually.

In today's world perhaps we could say that the Jewish leaders at that time were going through the motions of traditional religious daily lives but they had forgotten the significance of true belief and faith. Are we in danger of following this example of yesterday's Jewish leaders?

Prayer: Lord Jesus, today and every day, renew my faith. This world is busy I sometimes I am tired. I get through the day with exhaustion. Renew my faith, trust and love for You. Fill me with your Spirit.

Lord, burst into my life anew and let others see You through my life today and every day. Amen.

Jesus healed the blind man. A man blind from birth. And yet, He was criticized for working on the Sabbath. They did not believe the blind man had been healed and ridiculed Him and yet stated proudly that they were disciples of Moses.

They knew the prophecies of the coming Messiah. They refused the evidence in front of their own eyes when they refused to believe this miracle even though they brought the blind man's parents to confirm the man was born blind.

And yet, they still refused to believe. They should have rejoiced in the healing miracle of the blind man who could now see. Were they too blind in their own ambitions, in their own power or position in life? The miracles that Jesus did were signs that He was from God. Many refused to acknowledge His power.

And yet I must acknowledge my own weakness. If I had lived in those days, who I would have followed? Would I have followed Jesus upon seeing His miracles or signs? Would I have taken a wait and see attitude or would I have followed the conventional religious leaders of the day and trusted in them? What would you have done?

Prayer: Lord, heal the eyes of my heart and remove the scales from my eyes to see You in my life today and each day anew. Do not allow this world to blind me to Your never-ending presence. Help me to see Your hands at work in my life and in those of Your people.
Help me live in the reality of Your love that you freely bestowed on Your people. Amen.

In the first part of this chapter, Jesus states He is the good shepherd. He says the sheep follow Him because they know His voice. Then in verse 15 He states, "I lay down My life for the sheep" (NASB).

Jesus' disciples did not seem to understand the full implications of what He was saying. It seems easy to say that we would give everything to those we love. We tend to use these types of words lightly. But Jesus was saying exactly what He knew He would do. He would lay down His life, He would die out of His love for you and me.

Jesus not only died for our sins He also rose again to care for His sheep. He rose from the dead and is alive today and evermore. He cares for His sheep. He cares for you and me today and tomorrow. If He died for us, He has not left us along but continues to care for us, His sheep.

Jesus also said the shepherd leads the sheep and they follow him because they know the voice of the shepherd.

Today, are we following the voice of the Shephard who laid down His life for us?

Prayer: Lord, open my ears that I may hear. Open my heart that I may follow. Open my eyes that I may see. Thank you for your love for me. You died for Your sheep. You live to care for Your sheep.

Lord, help me to follow you today and every day. Amen.

Jesus raises Lazarus!

Martha and Mary loved Jesus and had faith in them. They knew Jesus had health others during His ministry. They knew that if Jesus had been there before Lazarus died that Jesus could have and would have healed him. That is why they sent for Jesus when their brother became sick. And yet, I am sure they did not understand why Jesus waited and did not come to them immediately.

Jesus had power over creation. He turned water into wine. He had power over sickness and healed others. He made the blind to see. He spoke so differently than the religious leaders of the day.

And yet, Mary and Martha still had much to learn and grow in faith. They would see the power of Jesus as well as many others. Jesus had and has the power over death itself.

Lazarus had been dead 4 days!

And yet, Jesus raises Lazarus. While others could move the stone away, only Jesus could speak out and cause Lazarus to come from the grave.

And yet, because of His miracles the religious leaders still set out to kill Jesus. Why could they not see Jesus the way Mary and Martha saw Him?

Who will we follow today? This Jesus or others who cannot seem to understand that Jesus was and is of God and is continuing to have cause His kingdom to burst into this world. May we be like Joshua and say: "As for me and my house, we will follow the Lord" (Joshua 23:15 NASB).

Prayer: Lord, open our eyes to see the truth that is not evident in the world. Help us see with fresh eyes and a renewed heart the reality of your strength, power and love that can only be seen as You reveal it to us. At times we can only see what the world presents to us. Help us to be transformed by Your very presence and allow Your presence to be seen to others through us.

"Father, glorify Thy name" (John 12:29 NASB).

This should be our daily prayer. That the Father should be glorified in us.

Read the passage before this particular verse. Jesus is predicting His death. By this, the Father is glorified. In verse 24 Jesus states that a grain of wheat must fall to the earth and die to bear fruit. In the next verse, He states that anyone who loves their life loses it and anyone who hates his life in this world will have eternal life. Transforming thoughts.

Then Jesus says in verse 26 that if we are to serve Him, we must follow Him.

Then Jesus, after predicting His death, says "Father, glorify They name".

We must count all as lost to follow Him. There is no comparison. To follow Him and be within His presence now and forever more is the only way to life. I must die to self to live with Him. We must think that radically. Is all the world worth more than the presence of the Savior who loved us so much He died for us? Or are the temporary worldly goods worth more than life today, tomorrow and forever with our loving God.

Prayer: Lord, help me know the love, strength and power of Your presence each and every day. May I dedicate all I am to You. May Your love for me exhibited on the cross be my guide. May the richness of Your love be my blanket and shield.

Jesus washes the disciple's feet.

No, it should never be.

We should wash His feet.

The Son of God, the Creator of all that is, showed us an example of love and service. He taught us to put the needs of others first. He came to serve the Father and to give Himself for us. He was the greatest of all and yet not only washed their feet but died for their sins and our sins. He loved us and desired our companionship. He came to die for us so that by His act, His grace, we can live today, tomorrow and forever with Him.

Jesus goes on in verse 34 to give us a new commandment "that you love one another, even as I have loved you" (NASB).

The Giver of all life demonstrates His love and service. He then gives a new command that we are to love one another just as He loved us. He loved us so much He came and died for us on the cross.

How can we not be thankful?

Prayer: Lord, I am so imperfect. Help me to love You more each day. Teach me to serve as You served. Teach me to love as You love. Help me to give of myself as You gave Yourself. Help me to love and serve You and others.

What a marvelous chapter to focus on.

Jesus says He is in the Father and the Father is in Him. The Father abides in Him. He promises to send the "Helper, that He may be in you forever" (vs 17 NASB).

Here Jesus says what we sometimes do not pay enough attention to. In verse 20 He states we will "know that I am in My Father, and you in Me and I in you" (NASB).

Wow. Remember we are talking about the Creator, the One through Whom all was created. Think of Genesis 1 and John 1. He is the One who came out of love for us to die on the cross so that we can live today and forever with Him. This is the One who in Revelations says, "I am the Alpha and the Omega" (the first and the last) "who is and who was and who is to come, the Almighty" (Rev 1:8).

This is the One who states that "I am in the Father, and you in Me and I in you (vs. 20 NASB). This is the One who lives in us and us in Him. Oh, how can it be?

He sends His Holy Spirit to abide in us. We need a renewed sense of awe, of wonder, of being filled with love and thankfulness that He desires wo abide in us and for us to abide in Him. The Creator of the universe and all the stars we see at night loves us to desire us to live with Him forever and died on the cross and rose again to make that happen. May I always be inspired and in awe of this fact.

Prayer: Lord, sometimes we take being a "Christian" for granted. Help us to remain in awe that You choose to love us and to abide in us. Help us to remember how special it is to have the presence of your Spirit within us and to show the world a different way with You.

Wow. There is so much we could talk about in John 15. We could write a book discussing this chapter in detail.

Let's focus on some thoughts from this chapter for today.

In verse 9, Jesus says that He loves us just as the Father loves Him. Think about this for a minute. How great a love is this that He has for us. How can this be? He has chosen to love us.

Jesus then tells us to "abide" in His live. To live in His love. To stay in His love.

What does this mean? How can we do this? This seems too idealistic.

First, He tells us this means to keep His commandments. But wait, this turns out to be different than what we may think. He says in verse 12 that "This is My commandment, that you love one another as I have loved you" (NASB).

He then goes on to define this love by stating that this love means sacrifice, laying down one's life for their friends. Jesus is also looking here to His own death for us, His friends. He loves us so much He died for us.

How do we abide in His love? By obeying His commandment to love others as He has loved us. Giving of ourselves is the greatest expression of love. And we do this because He first loved us and gave Himself for us.

Prayer: *Jesus, help me to abide in Your love by obeying Your commandment to love others as You love me. I do this not out of obligation but in thankfulness because You have first loved me and gave Yourself for me so that I could live with you today and forever. Thank you for calling me Your friend.*

In this chapter Jesus continues to prepare His disciples for the fact that he will leave this world and will not be with them physically. However, He states that it is to their advantage because He will then send the "Helper" (vs 7 NASB). Who is this Helper? It is the Holy Spirit. He is God the Spirit, the third person of the trinity. In verse 13, Jesus states the Holy Spirit will guide them into the truth.

Jesus is not leaving His disciples alone. He is sending the Holy Spirit to be with them and within them. We think of the day of Pentecost. We can begin to think of the beginning of the worldwide Church. We know that He gives the Holy Spirit to indwell within us.

Jesus did not leave His disciples alone and He has not left us alone. He is with us and within us. He desires our companionship and has given us the Holy Spirit to be our "Helper".

Do you feel alone, that He is far away, that He has forgotten you? No, He loved you so much He died for you and has now given His Holy Spirit to guide us from today through eternity. He is as close to you as your own heart and soul.

Invite Him into your "heart-house" today anew.

Prayer: Lord, thank you for the gift of life with You and Your presence in our lives today through the Holy Spirit. Keep us within Your arms and within Your grasp. Help us to know Your presence with us even though at times regardless of outside circumstances. Thank you for sending us the Helper.

We have spoken about eternal life. That sounds so far off. So distant. It's not for today. It's sounds so far in the future.

No, Jesus says it is today. But what is it?

It is indeed today. Listen to the words of Jesus Himself. In verse 3 He says, "And this is eternal life, that they may know Thee, the only true God, and Jesus Christ whom Thou hast sent" (NASB).

Jesus is not talking about tomorrow or what happens after death but now…. today…. each day. Jesus came for you and me so that He could draw us to Himself. He has made us companions with Him. He calls us "friend". This daily companionship is possible. He cares for us, our circumstances. He says to come and be within His company.

And yet, Jesus has said He was leaving His disciples. Jesus prays for His disciples to the Father. And then he says" I do not ask in behalf of these alone, but for those also who believe in Me through their word" (vs.20). And then He takes it one step further by saying "that they may be in Us, that the world may believe that Thou didst send me (vs 21). Here He is saying we are one with Him and gives the mission to spread His love to others.

Prayer: Lord, thank you for your love, for drawing me to You and thank you for your companionship. It amazes me that You, the Creator, loves me so much to be my daily companion. How can I express my gratitude? Help me to allow You to live through me, to love through me and to help fulfill Your mission through me. Lead me, guide me, be my daily companion.

Here, let's discuss 2 thoughts from this chapter as we move towards Christ's death on the cross.

First, Jesus knew what was to happen. He and the Father are one and He knew the plan included his death on the cross for you and for me. In verse 4 it states that Jesus knew but "went forth" (NASB) and asked those who had come to take him away who they were seeking. He knew God's plan and did not deny, run or seek shelter from what was to come. He went forth and faced it. He would not deny or run from God's plan. May we never shrink from going forth and doing what He would desire us to do. We may not know how, but we must do what He wants us to do.

Secondly, the religious leaders would not enter to Praetorium in order that they may not become unclean according to the ceremonial law of the Jews. And yet, it is clear their whole purpose was to put Jesus to death. They wanted to put to death the One who is the author of life itself. What a contradiction. They thought they were doing a service to God. They had to outward appearance of religion with none of the substance of what a follower of God is truly about. They preached their truth but did not know the truth.

Prayer: *Lord, help me to see You and Your will for my life. Help me to go forth to do what you would have me to do. Help me remember you went forth due to Your love for us and help me to have only that motive as I move forth to do Your will. Help me to know You and forsake all forms of religion that do not conform to Your love and truth.*

Here the Jewish leaders again conspire to kill Jesus. Now they conspire with the hated occupiers, the Romans, and say they have no king but Caesar. Should they have not said they have no king but God?

Once again, we marvel how they failed to accept the signs Jesus performed openly to the crowds. He healed people and raised the dead. How could they not see and accept these signs? Did they ignore them? No, they talked to the blind man who was healed as well as his parents. Did they choose to reject them? If so, how do they reject the miracles as from anyone but God? Perhaps they were the blind ones themselves. They saw the signs and rejected them in disobedience.

Here we also see Pilate saying in verse 4 that he finds no guilt in Jesus and in verse 12 it states that he wanted to release Jesus, yet he yielded to the crowds. While he found no guilt in Jesus perhaps, he was trying to avoid personal guilt of his involvement in killing Jesus. However, after two thousand years and for eternity his guilt is recorded and known.

Prayer: *My Lord and Savior, thank you for salvation brought by the cross. Help me always accept the invitation into Your presence each and every day. Help me to heed Your signs, recorded in Your word and those you have performed in my life. Do not let me ignore or reject them. Help me to avoid the deceit of trying to avoid blame for not doing what You would have me to do. Fill me with Your Spirit to follow Your will and Your ways no matter what the cost. Let the light of Your Love so shine through me that You draw others to Yourself.*

Mary cried. She believed others had taken away the body of her Lord. She was crushed and the disciples met behind closed doors because of the fear of the Jewish authorities.

Such are we without the living Christ. We are hopeless and fearful. We have no chance of salvation and life everlasting with Him.

But wait. The real-life story is not over. Jesus is risen. He is risen indeed. He is with us and among us. He lives. He lives within us. He is not dead but alive. As he announces in Rev. 1:17-18 (NASB):"Do not be afraid; I am the first and the last, and the living One; and I was dead, and behold, I am alive forevermore, and I have the keys of death and of Hades." (NASB).

We need not be afraid or disillusioned. Indeed it is those who don't recognize Him who are disillusioned because they do not recognize the fact, the reality, that Jesus loves them, died for them, paid their entire debt for our sins, and conquered death so we can live with Him today, tomorrow and forever, Yes, we are invited into His presence. Will you accept the invitation into His presence in your daily life?

Prayer: *Lord Jesus, thank you for your love for me. A love that was so great that led to the cross so I can live with You and You in me today, tomorrow and forever. Remove the fear of following You even if we do not understand all Your ways. Lead us today into a closer walk with You.*

Peter had denied Jesus three times before His death on the cross. Oh, the guilt he must have carried and perhaps even more so after Jesus resurrection. He had denied his association with Jesus three times and yet he is loved by the Lord.

Yet here, Jesus loves Jesus and restores Him. He counters Peters three denials with the questions so Peter can reaffirm His love for Christ three times. He did not give up on Peter or disown Peter. How unlike us. What would I have done to someone who denied association with me? Would I ignore that individual or try to get even in some way? Not Jesus, He forgives and restores Jesus.

We know Peter accepts this forgiveness and becomes a leader among the disciples. We must also accept the forgiveness of Christ and go on to do His will.

Prayer: Lord, how we yearn to be more of what You want us to be. Lead us, guide us, forgive us and help us to accept Your forgiveness to move forward with newness of life in Your presence each and every day.

ABOUT THE AUTHOR

David Eakin has loved the Gospel of John and longed to write a devotional on the marvelous witness of the life of Christ. He completed an undergraduate degree in Theology and during his final year was awarded the Outstanding Achievement in the Study of Theology at Southwestern Assemblies of God University. He subsequently decided to pursue a Masters of Divinity at Wartburg Theological Seminary.

Lightning Source UK Ltd.
Milton Keynes UK
UKHW050307140820
367999UK00008BA/118